ROUTE 66

BY MARIA NELSON

Gareth Stevens
PUBLISHING

Please visit our website, www.garethstevens.com. For a free color catalog of all our high-quality books, call toll free 1-800-542-2595 or fax 1-877-542-2596.

Library of Congress Cataloging-in-Publication Data

Names: Nelson, Maria, author.
Title: Route 66 / Maria Nelson.
Description: New York : Gareth Stevens Publishing, [2017] | Series: Road
  trip: famous routes | Includes index.
Identifiers: LCCN 2016015492 | ISBN 9781482446722 (pbk.) | ISBN 9781482446715 (library bound) | ISBN
9781482449488 (6 pack)
Subjects: LCSH: United States Highway 66–History–Juvenile literature. |
  Automobile travel–United States–Juvenile literature.
Classification: LCC F595.3 .N45 2016 | DDC 917.304–dc23
LC record available at https://lccn.loc.gov/2016015492

First Edition

Published in 2017 by
Gareth Stevens Publishing
111 East 14th Street, Suite 349
New York, NY 10003

Copyright © 2017 Gareth Stevens Publishing

Designer: Andrea Davison-Bartolotta
Editor: Kristen Nelson

Photo credits: Cover, p. 1 (top) Ovidiu Hrubaru/Shutterstock.com; cover, p. 1 (bottom) Francesco Ferrarini/
Shutterstock.com; pp. 4, 21 (map) Rainier Lesniewski/Shutterstock.com; p. 5 trekandshoot/Shutterstock.com; p. 6
Al Freni/The Life Images Collection/Getty Images; p. 7 Car Culture Collection/Getty Images; p. 8 Mark Williamson/
Photolibrary/Getty Images; p. 9 David McNew/Getty Images; p. 11 (main) Denise Taylor/Moment Mobile/Getty
Images; p. 11 (inset) Tupungato/Shutterstock.com; p. 12 Rudy Balasko/Shutterstock.com; p. 13 Gimas/Shutterstock.com;
p. 15 (main) John Elk/Lonely Planet Images/Getty Images; p. 15 (inset) Richard Cummins/Lonely Planet Images/Getty
Images; p. 16 Rich Reid/National Geographic/Getty Images; p. 17 Josemaria Toscano/Shutterstock.com; p. 19 (main)
Nagel Photography/Shutterstock.com; p. 19 (inset) George Burba/Shutterstock.com; p. 20 (main) Jon Bilous/
Shutterstock.com; p. 20 (sign) elenaburn/Shutterstock.com; p. 21 (whale) Carol M. Highsmith/LOC.gov; p. 21 (cars)
BedoMedo/Shutterstock.com.

Printed in the United States of America

CPSIA compliance information: Batch #CS16GS: For further information contact Gareth Stevens, New York, New York at 1-800-542-2595.

Contents

Words in the glossary appear in **bold** type the first time they are used in the text.

Main Street of America

One of the most famous **routes** in US history doesn't exist anymore! Route 66 once connected Chicago, Illinois, and Los Angeles, California, running through several states and big cities. It was such an **iconic** roadway, people wrote about it in books, movies, and songs. Today, only parts of it have been **preserved**.

Luckily for road trippers, the path of this national historic highway is still easy to follow. There's so much to do, you'll need more than one road trip to do it all!

US Highway 66 was the official name of Route 66, but it was also called the "mother road" and the "Main Street of America."

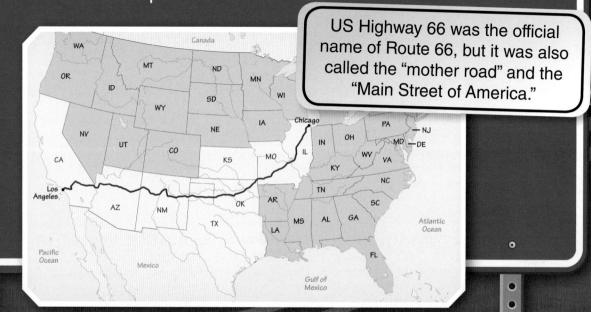

where found: crosses Illinois, Missouri, Kansas, Oklahoma, Texas, New Mexico, Arizona, California

year established: planning began in 1925; completed in 1938

year decommissioned: 1985

length: more than 2,000 miles (3,220 km)

periods of highest traffic: 1930s when those who lived in the **Dust Bowl** traveled west; late 1940s following World War II (1939–1945)

major attractions: Chain of Rocks Bridge, London Bridge, the Painted Desert, **Petrified** Forest National Park, Santa Fe National Forest, the Will Rogers Memorial Museum, Chicago, Los Angeles

Pit Stop

Nat King Cole was the first to tell people to "get their kicks" in the famous song called "Route 66."

The Growth of Route 66

In 1925, the US government decided to build a system of roads across the nation. A route connecting Chicago and Los Angeles was part of this plan from the start. First called Route 60, then Route 62, the roadway was finally named Route 66.

The eight states it ran through had to build their own length of the route, so it wasn't completed until 1938. By then, many people were leaving the Dust Bowl for California. They used the new road to get there!

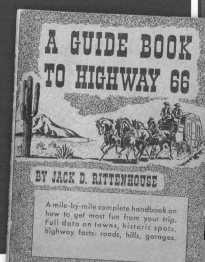

A GUIDE BOOK TO HIGHWAY 66

BY JACK D. RITTENHOUSE

A mile-by-mile complete handbook on how to get most fun from your trip. Full data on towns, historic spots, highway facts: roads, hills, garages.

Pit Stop

People traveling Route 66 needed food, gas, and places to stay. So, hotels, gas stations, and many of the first fast-food restaurants began to be built along the roadway during the 1930s.

Have you ever seen a billboard as you were driving? Advertising to drivers on a road became popular with Route 66!

Highways Take Over

By the mid-1950s, Route 66 and other major roadways across the United States were dealing with more cars than they could handle. Wider, safer roads were built, and they bypassed parts of Route 66. Then, the US government started to construct high-speed superhighways. These were often right next to the old roadway or built over parts of it.

By 1984, the last bit of Route 66 that was being used was bypassed by new highways. In June 1985, the route was officially decommissioned.

Pit Stop

Just as highways bypassed Route 66, Route 66 had taken the place of old auto trails that people once used to travel across America.

In 1990, the US government passed a law stating that Route 66 was a **symbol** of America's past that should be preserved. You can visit parts of the original road, though parts of it aren't in good shape.

Remembering Route 66

What better place to start a Route 66 road trip than Chicago? Visitors to Chicago, one of the biggest cities in the United States, can enjoy beautiful Grant Park or look out on Lake Michigan from the top of the Ferris wheel at Navy Pier.

Heading southwest from Chicago along the historic path of Route 66 is Pontiac, Illinois, home to the Route 66 Association Hall of Fame & Museum. The museum has Route 66 **memorabilia** and great facts about the history of the roadway and traveling it today.

Along Route 66's historic path, road trippers will find many stores and museums that sell or show collectibles related to Route 66 and its past.

Navy Pier

Chain of Rocks Bridge

In order to pass from Illinois to Missouri while on a road trip, you'll have to cross the Mississippi River. One way to do this in the past was by the Old Chain of Rocks Bridge, which was built with a 22-degree bend in the middle!

Today, you can only cross the old bridge on foot or by bike. Found close to St. Louis, Missouri, the bridge is also the beginning of a path that ends at the famous St. Louis Gateway **Arch**!

Pit Stop

The Gateway Arch is 630 feet (192 m) tall! Visitors can travel up to the observation deck at the top of the arch and see out over the city.

FREE RADIO & TV
66
AUTO COURT
NO VACANCY
66
EAT
TEXACO

Just as new highways bypassed Route 66, the Old Chain of Rocks Bridge was bypassed in 1967 when the New Chain of Rocks Bridge was constructed.

13

Museum Tour

Have you ever wanted to learn how to rope a cow like a cowboy? You can in Claremore, Oklahoma, at the Will Rogers Memorial Museum. As a young man, Will Rogers worked as a cowboy. He was great at rope tricks that you can try to learn at the museum!

Science Museum Oklahoma in Oklahoma City will test your daring, too, with a two-story tree house you can climb into! The museum also includes places to learn about space and building a race car.

Pit Stop

The makers of the movie *Cars* visited Route 66 for **inspiration**. The character of Sally Carrera is based on the owner of the Rock Café in Stroud, Oklahoma—another place you can stop on your road trip!

Will Rogers is best known for being a famous actor and newspaper writer during the 1930s. You can see his bedroom, shown here, at the memorial museum! Sometimes Route 66 is called Will Rogers Highway.

"I never met a man I didn't like"

WILL ROGERS
1879 - 1935

15

Southwest Cities

Route 66 passes through the northern Texas city of Amarillo. Here, you can drive on the original Route 66! Amarillo is also home to the Kwahadi Museum of the American Indian. Depending on when you visit, the museum puts on different **traditional** Pueblo dances on Friday and Saturday nights.

Santa Fe, New Mexico, can be an adventurous road trip stop! Go hiking or climbing in Las Conchas canyon in Santa Fe National Forest, take a hot air balloon ride, or go white-water rafting on the Rio Grande!

Visitors can find out a lot about the rich history of the southwestern United States in Albuquerque, New Mexico. People first settled Old Town Albuquerque in 1706!

Natural Beauty

There are many national parks not far from the path of old Route 66, including the Grand Canyon! Near the New Mexico border in Arizona is Petrified Forest National Park. Here you can see the petrified remains of trees that were buried in dirt, plant remains, and ash from a **volcano** more than 200 million years ago!

The park is part of the Painted Desert. Here, wind and weather have shaped rock into an odd landscape, **revealing** layers of colorful rock you have to see to believe are real!

Pit Stop

In the middle of the Arizona desert sits London Bridge, which was built across the Thames River in London, England, in the 1830s. When a newer bridge replaced it, a builder bought the old bridge and put it across part of the Colorado River in the late 1960s!

Pieces of petrified wood from the park look like crystals and can be many pretty colors.

19

California

Route 66 ended in sunny Los Angeles. Called the "City of Angels," Los Angeles is one of the largest cities in the world! It isn't far from the Pacific Ocean and is near many famous beaches, including the Santa Monica Pier and Venice Beach. Another great road trip route, the Pacific Coast Highway, runs right past LA, too!

Would you like to travel Route 66? There's a lot more to explore near this iconic roadway, so buckle up and hit the road!

SANTA MONICA

66

End of the Trail

20

Santa Monica has more than just a beach. It has an aquarium, a carousel, and even a roller coaster!

Weird and Wacky on Route 66

Tulsa Tripper
Afton, Oklahoma
A man-sized penguin stands inside the Afton Station.

McDonald's Museum
San Bernardino, California
This museum is where the first McDonald's restaurant was built!

Blue Whale
Catoosa, Oklahoma
Visitors can climb into the mouth of a huge concrete whale!

Chicago

Los Angeles

Cadillac Ranch
Amarillo, Texas
See almost a dozen Cadillacs sticking out of the ground!

Harrell House of Natural Oddities
Santa Fe, New Mexico
See dinosaur bones, or even feed a tarantula!

Glossary

arch: a curved form

decommission: to remove from service

Dust Bowl: parts of Oklahoma, Kansas, and Texas that had bad dust storms in the 1930s because of lack of rain and poor farming practices

iconic: being widely recognized

inspiration: something that causes someone to want to do something

memorabilia: things that show remembrance of a time or place

petrify: to change to stone

preserve: to keep something in its original state

reveal: to open up to view

route: a course that people travel

symbol: something that stands for something else

traditional: having to do with long-practiced ways of life

volcano: an opening in a planet's surface through which hot, liquid rock sometimes flows

For More Information

Books

Dillard, Sheri. *What's Great About Oklahoma?* Minneapolis, MN: Lerner Publications Company, 2015.

Price, Sean. *Route 66: America's Road.* Chicago, IL: Raintree, 2008.

Websites

National Historic Route 66 Federation
national66.org
See old pictures and read stories about what life was like along Route 66 in the past.

Route 66 Map
nps.gov/nr/travel/route66/maps66.html
Is part of old Route 66 near you? Check this map!

Route 66 Trivia, Facts and Figures
theroute-66.com/trivia.html
Find out lots of fun facts about Route 66.

Index